The Time We Turned

THE SHEARSMAN CHAPBOOK SERIES, 2014

Martyn Crucefix *The Time We Turned*
Patricia Debney *Gestation*
juli Jana *ra-t*
Anthony Rudolf *Go into the Question*
Robert Vas Dias *Arrivals and Departures*

The Time We Turned

New Poems

Martyn Crucefix

Shearsman Books

First published in the United Kingdom in 2014 by
Shearsman Books
50 Westons Hill Drive
Emersons Green
BRISTOL
BS16 7DF

Shearsman Books Ltd Registered Office
30–31 St. James Place, Mangotsfield, Bristol BS16 9JB
(this address not for correspondence)

www.shearsman.com

ISBN 978-1-84861-368-3

Contents

The map house
for D.T.

I

When I knew him I knew him in the city
then in this northern town

there he was walking towards me
still balding aggressively though slate-grey tufts

and corkscrews the colour of the skies
on that morning above the fells

proliferated over and round his ears—
there beside him the son I'd never seen

though by then he was already six years old
and that morning already two Easters ago

II

We lost touch yet I know why he comes
to mind now that we have settled

if temporarily in this house whose owner
has decked it with maps of all kinds

both upstairs and down—so from this sofa
I might triangulate the distance

from York to Berwick-on-Tweed
or between my youth and two universities

might trace an absentminded finger
across the bulbous relief of Wales

even along the network of paths that run
between our local lake our local fells

III

One of those evenings we met in the city
he confessed his love of the thrill

of standing on the ground floor of Stanfords
on Long Acre of being surrounded

by maps and globes and charts in books
maps unbound in shallow pull-out drawers

maps rolled in cylinders or displayed on cords
those gleaming plasticated lumpen reliefs

of the least populated regions of the world
of foothills mountains deserts littorals

IV

He wrote of it or perhaps we simply talked
across the table spills—some way

he made it clear what really excited him
was not the length or breadth of a map

but it's other hidden dimension—
he'd wave a hand and shake greying curls

and indicate something almost lost
in a corner somewhere squirreled away

like a tiny after-thought or like a coin
of the smallest denomination

something always there if you look for it—
standing before a framed ink-sketch map

of this northern town I hear him again
it's time you fool—the date don't you see?

V

Still obedient after all these years
I squint into each framed corner in turn

but grow distracted at the surface of things
end up tracing a walk we took last night

along Rawling Street past the iron gates
of St Mary's and across the car park

to Crow Park and the lake where happily
we took far longer than we'd planned

leaning on those blue-painted railings
running above the little brown-shingled strand

where every evening pleasure-boats for hire
are beached and roped one to the other

VI

The sun fell bright toward the black hill
we've not yet learned to name and we cursed

ourselves for not having a camera—
it felt a moment worth the preservation

especially as across the flat-clean calm
like the glassy delusion of another world

a red-painted dinghy drove to the beach
its sails furled its sleepily-turning outboard

cutting suddenly though the little hull
possessed enough momentum still

to drive it securely to the yellow shingle
where two figures worked to make her safe

VII

It was that instant the sun's disc dropped
behind the hill—light cut theatrically

and the temperature plummeted too
as we turned back toward the narrow streets

and if I could explain anything of this
walking on Long Acre or through Golden Square

or with his son along some wind-swept beach
I'd want to tell it right—some obscurely-

inherited sense of debt or what promise is it
we make to those we hardly see for years—

I'd want to say it was past seven o'clock
or perhaps by then even seven-fifteen—

I'm sure of it now—a quarter past the hour
was the time we turned and part of what it meant

A thousand chattering images

in memory of Larry Levis

I

I read them all hours—the weather signs
beyond the loose rattle of single panes
where a single glance
suggests horizontal flakes
in the exterior churning of a great machine

that refuses to ease
till it has forced my retreat
off the mountain-edge before eleven o'clock—
a gale so determined and cold
it tips me into heather tufts beside the track

II

It persuades me to retreat to Patterdale
the car park of The White Lion
where I stand to wonder unexpectedly
if what I really need
is to make peace with myself man to boy

whether these forty years
in this futile search for equanimity
with that girl was my first
my biggest mistake because she still
re-appears occasionally in my dreams—

re-worked utterly with the years
tenderly I try to push back a lock
of her purple hair—

though even in the dream world
neither she nor I have anything left to say

III

Sit and number the iron waves
where they expire on the gentle gradient
of the lake's empty beach—
only to be reminded of a voice
a man years-dead but recently heard

with just some minor distortion
as he leans towards the microphone
to address his audience
some of whom have paid to listen
Hi there—can you hear me—I hope so

because we're recording for posterity—
good luck with that! you can? then here goes . . .
and the recital gets under way
his poetry circling back
on itself in a larger musical pattern

in which he works out those buried seams
of college days a friend lost in Vietnam
a painting and a smile
and his standing before
the black marble wall in Washington

IV

These weather signs—I read them all hours
as the waves come in
and so it must be as man to boy

though what the older has to say
to the younger still remains a mystery—

perhaps that happiness is this steady state
or that joy is this gale sweeping
down the lake and rippling everything
and I mean everything
so nothing seems capable of holding

its place for long but instead
I am content to squat on this grassy bank
beside this tinkling rill—
in hope he'd allow such self-conscious use
of Romantic language and hope

of course that you will too and on what
grounds could she ever object—
all the while the wind shreds itself
in the boughs of a pine above me
how it moans—how these noises modulate

in the lee of the wall yet curiously blend
with the robin's *tick-ticking*
in a shaking aspen and on the waters
that flow past my feet
a thousand chattering images of the reflected sun

V

So can you hear me—am I clear now
to the back and if you can hear
then will you forgive me for asking so much
for understanding too little
can you forgive me for settling for this

VI

Then I'll whisper the pleasures
of tracking the demise
of every wave on this shingle beach
its little six inch slapping
showing white at first against the metal-dark

then a rippling progress as each falls
the white emboldened cap
and then foaming it fades—
I'll whisper something of how each loses
colour then as quickly darkens back

to the dark of the body of the water
to come nibbling still up the beach
all the while clarifying to boast reds and blues
yellows and greens the colours
of a thousand stones that roll beneath my feet

VII

Then find words to explain the moment
waves come to be seen as the machine
we call time—how we're inclined to stop it
with our use of memory
only to set it in motion again in the act

of remembering the man the girl the boy
I was then though believing
still the quality of attention is enough to be
redeemed enough in the course
of this lovely wavering uneasy conversation

Sonnets for Rosalía de Castro

For Rosalía

Then sing out boy I'll bring you chestnuts
dumplings in broth and bread sopped in wine—
so Rosalía dares you from Padron
where the springs well up the pastures glow

between the grass and the grapevine
beneath the oak the fig the eucalyptus—
no better place to sing of all there is
whether it's bathed in flowers or swathed in mist

no sweeter language to sing bitter longings
the sigh of love or grief or mystery
the murmur of night after the long afternoons

and it's this she asks you and this alone
that you sing in a language you speak you praise
her country from the lips of your springs

O Farso

To begin with not clear what the lighthouse does
with its absence of glass lens and bulb
at least to the naked eye—
just a spindly array of instruments up top

above the disappointingly stubby column
on a cliff-top with its padlocked metal doorway—
but no sooner has the walking begun
than its subtle powers become obvious

your every step determined by its position
the heather the stony paths the steep incline
each locked in communication with it

and where all might have flowed before you
in a salted windswept wide plenitude
the lighthouse utters its singular word

The old man of Carballedo

Leaves the preordained gloom of her kitchen
for the garden where he finds nothing
but colours and every one welcome—
there he stirs earth's dusty August greys

the plain-handed greenery of the fig's leaves
the bone-like stalks of tall brassica
that he cuts and cuts and it comes again
the brown immobility of six brooding hens

the silver tints in the fingers of the olive
and by evening whatever colours persist
in his voice unearthed long ago committed

to heart as light fades to become a part
of the sun's darkening and caramelizing—
his singing shot through with the glitter of jet

At Santiago de Compostela

Awkward at what someone calls 'the holy end'
where the silver box of revered bones
is secure in its much-visited cellar
swept clean of course but surprisingly plain

beneath the mountainous eruption of golds—
of gold leaf of gold paint to trap the eye
you prefer to be spun round
to be accompanied to the dusty entrance

to lay fingers snugly in the marble niche
worn by millions who pressed there too
once they'd shaken the road from their shoes—

though of course it cannot be shaken off
no more than the familiar door the gate the roof
you turned from took one step and were gone

Rock drawings near Touron

The clever one who thought to delete time
the one who saw the running of the deer
yet saw it as if existing beyond the moment
and so excised all subtlety of light

of shade of angle of texture of motion—
so scraped it shallowly upon these rocks
clumsily in profile yet held on to it
with this handless grasp this sort of magic—

soon he progressed to the lights in the sky
this mild one filling the cool dark hours
this god-like one of daylight he then scratched

as deepening concentric circles of power
and knowledge of himself as his mind
zooms inwards and bound by bound expands

On the beach at night alone

The creaming of the clockwork surf is nothing—
its coils and ringlets returning small meals
of feather and fragments of weed
since your wish now is to find a medium

more dense than air a medium closer
to your own body to find it to release yourself
till you are buoyed up
your mind almost wholly extinguished

to recover a place perhaps even the oldest place—
just one small circuit firing in fear
of this great mother whose mathematical heart

pulses seven then seven once more lucky seven
till you begin to understand how she
can add you and still contrive to make one

Tuesday market at Pontecandelas

The thought persists how there must
have been one whose nose was less buried
in the trough of what is passing
the pure of colours and of stinks and shapes

so he might have stood there an instant
in his own field of vision and been capable
in such self-divorce of seeing
advantages a better way a quicker way—

proved right it will have been his own children
who grew taller healthier better fed
and so the next generation stood there too

gathering gestures words abstracting ideals
ideology till a world was constructed
chaff fell by the wayside evil was invented

The tyrant born in Ferrol

Though from these parts they could not
persuade him to love the specifics the springs
at the roadside the cock's crow the scum on lagoons
the shadows cast under a mare's ribs—

he'd rather deny the dust between his toes
since he preferred the idea that refuses to die
of shaping his country in his own image
willing even to trample his own language—

now he's dead and this adolescent gull
you find shivering in the shade of the marina wall
is ready to die like nothing you've seen

yet still he thrusts his mini iPad towards it
snaps then saunters along the jetty
composing a caption you guess he's terrifying

Your mother in remission at Mogor

The new moon-like curve of the paring of the beach
is groomed at night—only the chaotic doodling
of gulls that stalk and scavenge
mark it these mornings scudding high and blue

above the currents of the sheltered *rivas*
moving so flat and calm they seem to have lost
all knowledge of waves of the shaggy oceans
that roll forever at their turned backs—

it's here she walks with such clear purpose
as if towards a settled conclusion
but really turning back before the rock pools

pushing the day like a bow wave before her
she paces for hours beside the curved water's edge
wearing it down as the tide retreats

At the Fonte da Lena

Like cream or like butter but this is water
from a wound in the hillside above the house
where the parish church is shuttered
the portraits on its tombs locked under glass

mostly young and smartly attired for their day—
yet what lay before them is like water
dribbling into this trough with its micro-climates
dank with valerian and drooping fern and slugs—

across the road you prefer this consoling scene
of two parents staked under the midday sun
seeming content with the scrubby grass

he's badged and alone the ring through his nose
while she's rope-lassoed about the horns
while two youngsters are clearly free to roam

Sunbathing beyond Hio

Oiled bodies sprawl on the beach at midday
the sun's wheel drives itself through the sky—
invisibly it drives us too
from a distance whoever knows what it is

yet one thing you know is it's not enough
to picture it as a plain circle whether written
on rock paper sand water—it must be
a whole series of one nestling within the next

to suggest something of its power
in such hoops and in zeroing them down
there's the thrill of moving closer to the source

of whittling it to something it cannot be
at the same time heightening what it is until
you're panting after something pornographic

Two weddings at Soutomaior

You stand behind battlements and arrow-slits
while a different vision of life unrolls
its red carpets across the courtyard lawn
as events management dresses wooden chairs

in white outfits with love's scarlet bows
behind them—then steadies a portable crucifix
on an outdoor altar for nuptials
that will turn a blind eye to the granite caskets

propped against these walls—everything awaits
the promising couple while this earlier pair
have already made their vows and been applauded

their Picasso's bodywork flaunts its fleece
of yellow post-it notes its fluttering of tongues
to sing them past the rough and the smooth

79 *dead at A Grandeira*
25.7.13

You refuse to walk four grieving miles out of town
to find these two consoling each other
over friends or relatives or those wider circles
of being human—they clutch one another

in a bitter harmony of coincidental greys
you notice as you turn the photograph—
each clasping a smart-phone they hoped would yield
better news—given up now—barely given up—

instead they see what the whole world has seen
the white nose of the beautiful train
appearing to make the bend beside the wall

then it tips with too much speed into history
leaving only the little things like a crushed bottle
a magazine torn wires hung from the ceiling

Livestock in Pozo Negro

The pasture she has been moved to is a fine one
far from the tarmac in the shade of two oaks
the grass here is tall and the thistles few
the sun will rise from behind the hill

she will have the pleasure of shade all morning
the long streaks of evening in which to wait—
then how to explain why you find her standing
crying all day as if ripped at the root

in such a big bovine lamentation—
why she cannot settle to new grass
but as she lets her head fall towards the earth

cocks her muzzle and begins to bellow
at two calf-shaped holes how many circles broken
she roars one to the other to another's shadow

In the woods above Rebordello

On the hill clothed thickly with sweet chestnut
oak and eucalyptus once upon a time
this house defined itself in local granite
in all kinds of local wood in wrought iron

snug-fitting and well-pointed and rectangular
for a while there were creatures for whom
this was a locale a self-definition
a series of taken-for-granted interiors—

awash now with remembrance as you loiter
the gate off its hinges and every floorboard rotted
to nothing even the stone staircase

silted rich and overgrown is like a slipway
to an ocean in place of events the long tides
of vegetation return it to the primal flood-gates

After Rosalía

You sing and sing but it's not very graceful
as you were never—you regret this—a graceful child
would prefer your songs to be sweeter
you'd prefer them to flit like butterflies

or the spume of waves under the fleck of stars—
but on such occasions when grace falls short
then feeling must suffice
if not always enough to express what you wish

not ever enough—still it sounds as if you sing
and if it's true something eludes
that grace in singing's not within your reach

then love of small things must see you through—
what else can you do—O how unlucky you were
not to be born more graceful

Four trees fallen

I

Two hours into the walk
I recognise an idea that occurred
to me twenty years ago—
as I pass this tree up-turned
with its metres-wide plate
of spreading roots tipped fully
ninety degrees from the horizontal
so what lay underground
is now exposed to the air
this weather of rain and sleet
that bowls along on a wind
coming cold from the north—
I imagine it must have been
this same wind though perhaps
in the tempestuous pitch
of night that blew with such power
to topple a tree like this
to lever its roots up-turned
from almost immemorial dark
into the temporary dark
of one night's storm—if it was
at night—left exposed at dawn
to new sunlight to noon and sunset
to follow the wheeling lights
we're familiar with and up close
I see roots about the thickness
of my forearm and here's one
that how many decades ago
as it struck out for moisture
clutched this red flattish rock

and held on would not let go
even on the night of the storm—
if the storm blew at night

II

I'm sure it was on Port Meadow
more than twenty years ago—
I was walking with a girl
and the river high and brown
so perhaps it was springtime
or Michaelmas as we'd posture
it then and we came to a tree
laid on the grassy flood-plain
with its great dial of roots
arse over tip and on that occasion
I wanted to look close though
then I picked a white pebble
from the tangled nest of once-
subterranean wood with just
the vaguest of thoughts
about things being unearthed
of things long buried in the dark—
exactly the kind of reflections
I repeat today though across
the intervening decades
I can persuade myself
they come more clearly to me
though perhaps I'm wrong in that
as there are roots and branches
that lie buried too deep
and to come clear would take such
a storm by day or tempest by night
I'm sure they are seldom

the kind of thing I'd arrive at
through study or by a steady gaze
or might emerge with clarity
in the middle of casual talk

III

Walking on—and with each step
I remember a third fallen tree
this morning this one skirted
some miles back beside a stream
yet this other trunk bristled
weirdly with half-moons of coins
in its papery folds each hammered
by walkers till the coins were bent
and stressed from blows
of rocks needed to sink them deep
and this tree I also remember
was not the first of its kind—what
year was it what walk beside
what stream of whisky-brown waters
did I stand by a fourth fallen trunk
in that same way gleamingly
scaled with hundreds of coins—
some had planted light-hearted
coppers while others had
invested more heavily with silver
or the thick edges of pounds
and even two-pound coins—
I suppose just taking a breather
or something to amuse the kids
while others thought playfully
to placate the spirits of the place
with its damps and shades
and slippery rocks—perhaps to give

a gift that could never be spent
digging deep in their pockets
as I too hammered and thought
I might pay the fare for a journey
yet to be made to find my way
back to dispense with the need
for daylight tempests or storms
in the pitch of night to retrace
my steps to the original place
whether it might be noon or dusk
or rain or sun a decisive taking
back a preternatural reprise